Funny 4 God

☞ Rick Eichorn & Mike Webb ☜

TATE PUBLISHING *& Enterprises*

Dedication

To God,

Who gave us the talents to do His ministry

And for our wives,

Beth and Julie,

who have to put up with our silliness every

single day of the year.

Acknowledgements

As always, we owe a ton of gratitude to our wives and our families, who have to deal with many things alone while we are on the road ministering to others, and who continue to lift us up with their words of encouragement. They have always been there to support us every step of the way. Their acts of sacrifice for our ministry are way too many to count. We love them and thank God that He placed them in our lives.

Thank you to past members of the group: Bobby (Stumpy), Teri (Edna), Nellie (Mom), Tracy (the bratty sister), Chris, and Johnny. We also want to thank Matt for filling in during those times when we needed him. Thanks to all of you for helping build us to where we are today. We will always cherish the times we worked together and the laughter we shared.

Thank you to our church families and our friends, who lift us up and strengthen us in our daily walk with the Lord. You inspire us with the Word, hold us up in prayer, sacrifice your time and talents for us, but most importantly, through it all, love us for who we are anyway!

Table of Contents

Preface

Welcome to the Christian Comedy Caravan!

Job 8:21 "He will yet fill your mouth with laughter and your lips with shouts of joy."

Are you tired of hearing that Christians are boring? Or that they do not know how to have any fun or joy in their lives? I know we were.

For those of you who are not familiar with us, we are Mike Webb and Rick Eichorn of the Christian Comedy Caravan. In August of 1997, we combined our 30+ years of acting and theatrical experience into a unique blend of ministry and comedy. Using our passion for serving the Lord and bringing others to Christ, the Christian Comedy Caravan was born.

We have taken our message to many different venues throughout the United States, using a combination of prepared skits and improvisation to provide a light-hearted look at life as it applies to Scripture in today's society. A biblical message applies to each performance piece, dealing with a wide variety of topics such as faith, commitment, service, married or single life, worship, prayer, and a host of other biblical topics.

What follows in this book is a series of Christian comedy drama skits that will provide you with a different look into our spiritual walk through life. Most of the skits here can be used with a number of characters with limited props but can also be adapted to fit just two characters, like we have done. Everything else is up to you. The more creative you are and the bigger your imagination, the more fun you can have spreading the Gospel of Christ to everyone around you.

God has given us a gift to be able to make people laugh for the sake of His kingdom. We are not the best actors in the world today, but we are faithful to what God is having us do. We are very thankful for those opportunities He has given us and for the doors He has yet to open for us. We hope you enjoy this book of skits, using it to make others smile and learn a little bit more about God, and we hope to have the opportunity to come and minister to you in the future.

God bless you, and remember, there is always *joy* in the LORD!

Mike & Rick

The Ready-Made Christian
(an audience-participation infomercial)

Purpose

Too many of us get caught up in the image of Christianity and put on a good show so that we look good to our Christian friends. Scripture tells us that we need to focus instead on truly living a Christ-centered life. God sees what we do in private, and only He can give us the ultimate reward.

Running Time
7–10 minutes

Characters
Don Papaya: the host and self-proclaimed king of the infomercial

Kitty: Don's highly energetic assistant
Christian: the subject of Don's development
Announcer: off-stage voice

Costumes
Don, Kitty: any
Christian: business suit

Props
Bible
Box of white envelopes
Receipt booklet
Gold cross necklace
WWJD bracelet
Icthus

Application
This skit takes a look at some of the things we do as Christians to make ourselves look good to others. You will turn the venue into a live studio audience for the taping of the newest infomercial. You may want to set up the locale during the introduction. The sillier and more excited the performers can be in these characters, the more the audience will be able to see these flaws in themselves, which is, of course, the goal. The skit works very well if Christian is an unsuspecting member of the audience, perhaps a Pastor or lay leader of the host church.

Don is the ultimate salesman. As the king of the infomercial, he is known for developing products that the public will buy into. He is very excited about the product he is demonstrating, but his excitement is portrayed in a professional manner, as he does not want to compromise his potential sales.

Kitty is a very excitable assistant, somewhat ditzy. The more exaggerated the excitement can be portrayed, the more the skit will succeed. The excitement needs to be contagious as she gets the audience involved. There can be as much humor in the portrayal of these characters as there is in the script itself, and it will help emphasize the message.

As mentioned before, the character of Christian works well if played by a well-known member of the audience. While there are no lines for this character, the mere presence of Christian, especially if played by the right person, presents some good opportunities to improvise.

The announcer is needed at the end of the skit to recap the infomercial. If there is not another performer available, Kitty can present this part, or an audience member can be used to read a script.

Scripture Reference
Matthew 6:1–6

[1]"Be careful not to do your 'acts of righteousness' before men, to be seen by them. If you do, you will have no reward from your Father in heaven. [2]"So when you give to the needy, do not announce it with trumpets, as the hypocrites do in the synagogues and on the streets, to be honored by men. I tell you the truth, they have received their reward in full. [3]But when

you give to the needy, do not let your left hand know what your right hand is doing, ⁴so that your giving may be in secret. Then your Father, who sees what is done in secret, will reward you. ⁵"And when you pray, do not be like the hypocrites, for they love to pray standing in the synagogues and on the street corners to be seen by men. I tell you the truth, they have received their reward in full. ⁶But when you pray, go into your room, close the door and pray to your Father, who is unseen. Then your Father, who sees what is done in secret, will reward you.

Skit

(*Kitty comes to center stage and begins the infomercial with a lot of excitement.*)

Kitty: Good evening, and welcome to yet another amazing offer from the 'Image is Everything Company.' Yes, the same people that brought you the Soccer Mom, the Wall Street Man, and the Generation X-er have an amazing new offer for you. Have you ever been pressured by your Christian friends to go to church? Or felt out of place because you couldn't find a verse in the Bible? Well, our friend Don Papaya is back, and you won't believe what he has brought with him today. I'm so excited, let's not waste another minute. Ladies and gentlemen, please welcome the king of the infomercial, Don Papaya!

(*Kitty leads the audience in applause; Don makes a grand entrance to center stage.*)

Don: Thank you, Kitty, and welcome all. We at 'Image is Everything' are very excited about what we have developed. We have come up with a revolutionary new program that allows everybody to fit into the politically correct world of Christianity without any pressures or expectations.

Kitty: Are you serious? Tell our audience how this development came about.

Don: Well, Kitty, you see it all around us. People are going to church, reading their Bibles, all the things that make a good Christian. But more and more, you see people acting like Christians everywhere you go.

Kitty: I know what you mean. When was the last time you went through a whole day at work without getting one of those feel-good e-mails?

Don: Or got something in the mail trying to guilt you into sponsoring a child from a third-world country?

Kitty: So you're saying you've developed a way to be a Christian without the extra baggage!

Don: That's right, Kitty. We have developed the Ready-Made Christian. It's a revolutionary way that you can become a Christian without all of the pressures that come with living a Christian life.

Kitty: It sounds fabulous, Don! When can we see your latest masterpiece?

Don: Let's bring him out now. Ladies and gentlemen, let me present our latest development, Christian.

(*Don goes into the audience and brings an unsuspecting Christian to center stage*)

Don: As you can see, he is dressed in the latest style of (*type of clothing, i.e. business suit*), complete with (*color*) shirt and (*accessory, i.e. contemporary necktie*). Each time he enters a church, he will certainly turn heads.

Kitty: Very handsome, but what about the rest of the week? It's a lot of pressure to live a Christian life all the time.

Don: That's the best part. You don't have to act any differently the rest of the week than you do now. If you show up at church on Sunday, you're being seen by all of your Christian friends. Most of them never see you the rest of the week. And by passing a few e-mails at work, you'll have your coworkers convinced you're as dedicated as any Christian.

Kitty: Isn't that amazing, everybody?! (*Kitty leads the audience in applause.*) Now, Don, I know a lot of churches pressure their members to donate large sums of money, some as much as 10% of their income! Now, I know churches don't operate for free, but couldn't this get expensive for our ready-made Christian?

(*Kitty gives Christian a box of envelopes and a receipt booklet as Don makes his presentation.*)

Don: One might think, Kitty. But the beauty of this program is you can give the impression of making large donations without actually doing so. We even include a year's supply of offering envelopes and a book of receipts for your tax-free donations. Just drop an envelope into the collection plate with a small token. Nobody would ever know.

(*Kitty gives Christian a Bible.*)

Kitty: That is truly ingenious. Now, I notice Christian carrying a Bible. Wouldn't it be expected of him to read it and learn from it? I don't know about you, but I know I wouldn't have time to make such a commitment.

Don: Not at all. If Christian simply carries his Bible with him at selected times, such as to church, nobody will ever know that he's never read a Scripture.

Kitty: Wow! What else does Christian come with?

(Kitty puts a cross around Christian's neck as Don makes his presentation.)

Don: Kitty, we thought it was important that Christian had some accessories that identify him as a dedicated Christian. We have included a beautiful 14-carat gold-plated cross to wear around his neck.

Kitty: You see so many people wearing crosses. That seems so essential when creating a Christian. What else?

(Kitty puts a WWJD bracelet on Christian's wrist as Don makes his presentation.)

Don: We have included something that only the most serious Christians wear. It's a WWJD bracelet.

Kitty: What Would Jesus Do! You know, Don, I've seen people wearing those. That's so perfect. It really adds a personal touch.

(Kitty gives Christian an Icthus as Don makes his presentation.)

Don: That's not all! We've also included one of these self-adhesive fish symbols to attach to the back of Christian's car.

Kitty: Don, this keeps getting better. Now how much is all of this going to cost? It looks like a fortune.

Don: Au contraire. And you know it's getting good when

we start talking French. Kitty, you might consider this entire package a bargain at $200.00. But if you call now, you can have the Ready-Made Christian for five easy payments of $49.99.

Announcer / Kitty: The Ready-Made Christian comes complete with (*type of clothing*) to impress your church-going friends. You will also receive your very own Bible, a year's supply of offering envelopes and tax-free receipts, a 14-carat gold-plated cross to wear around your neck, a WWJD bracelet, and a self-adhesive fish to attach to the back of your car. All of this for 5 easy payments of $49.99. Get your credit cards ready. Operators are standing by. The toll-free number is 1–800-CHRISTIAN. That's 1–800-CHRISTIAN. Call now!

Don: Let me repeat that last part in case our audience went into shock. If you call now, you get this entire package for 5 east payments of $49.99. Get your credit cards ready. Just call 1–800-CHRISTIAN.

Kitty: Now Don, you have become legendary for the warranties you put on your developments. I have a feeling you've saved the best for last.

Don: You're absolutely right. Are you ready for this? The Ready-Made Christian comes with a lifetime guarantee! That's the entire time that you live on this earth!

Kitty: What do you say, folks? Call now!

Nothing But The Truth

Purpose

Study of the Word of God is an integral part of every Christian's walk with Christ. The Bible is the blueprint for how we are to live our lives, and it requires an understanding that we will only gain through intense study. The outside forces of today's society are strong, and we can easily be led astray if we are not equipped with God's Word.

Running Time

5–10 minutes

Characters

Dr. Dan: host of a radio talk show
Caller #1: off stage voice
Caller #2: off stage voice
Caller #3: off stage voice
Caller #4: off stage voice

Costumes

Dr. Dan: any

Props

Table
Chair
Microphone or headset

Application

This skit takes place in a radio studio, so the venue can be transformed into a live studio audience. Since the show is live, the performer on stage may take the liberty to interact with the audience.

Dr. Dan is a character that is clearly misinformed about Scripture and Christian principles. Since he is a performer by trade, he should assume the pretentious qualities of a typical radio personality.

The callers are off stage voices. If the number of people becomes an issue, performers can double up on these parts and use different voices to distinguish the characters. Or use audience members for the parts of the callers, giving them a script with the questions to ask. With this option, the performer on stage can have some fun with the callers, leading to some great improv moments.

Scripture Reference
James 1:22–25

[22]Do not merely listen to the word, and so deceive yourselves. Do what it says. [23]Anyone who listens to the word but does not do what it says is like a man who looks at his face in a mirror [24]and, after looking at himself, goes away and immediately forgets what he looks like. [25]But the man who looks intently into the perfect law that gives freedom, and continues to do this, not forgetting what he has heard, but doing it—he will be blessed in what he does.

Skit

(Dr. Dan is sitting at a table center stage.)

Dr. Dan: Okay, we're back from commercial, and you're here with Dr. Dan on "Nothing But the Truth," your daily question-and-answer show. Today, we're taking questions on everything under the sun; so if you have a question, and you need the truth, give us a call. Remember our slogan, "Go ahead and ask; we're never wrong." All of our lines are full, so let's get to Monica on line 1. Hello Monica, you're on the air.

Caller 1: Hello? Am I really on?

Dr. Dan: (*annoyed*) Yes, Monica. What's your question?

Caller 1: Oh, wow! I didn't think I would get on!

Dr. Dan: And you won't be on long if you don't have a question.

Caller 1: Oh, right. Well, I'm a first-time caller but a long-time listener, and I know you're big into the truth, but I want to know—do you always base your decisions on scriptural truth?

Dr. Dan: I try to. What's your question?

Caller 1: Well, I have a neighbor who has been out of work for quite a while, and we've been helping out whenever we can, but I just wanted to know just how much we really need to do so that we don't feel guilty.

Dr. Dan: You say your neighbor hasn't been working?

Caller 1: Right.

Dr. Dan: For how long?

Caller 1: I guess it's been a little less than a year.

Dr. Dan: A year? I'd say you're done.

Caller 1: Really?

Dr. Dan: Really.

Caller 1: But I know our pastor has been talking about how the Bible tells us to love our neighbors as ourselves, and I would never let my own family go hungry.

Dr. Dan: Well, the Bible also says that God helps those that help themselves—right?

Caller 1: Actually, I don't think that's in the Bible . . .

Dr. Dan: Sure it is. I think it's in Hezekiah or something. Yeah, that's it.

Caller 1: Really?

Dr. Dan: Of course. Remember, we're never wrong. Thanks for your call—You're here with Dr. Dan on Nothing But the Truth. Hello, caller?

Caller 2: Yes, Dr. Dan?

Dr. Dan: Go ahead, you're on the air.

Caller 2: Yes, I was wondering, I have a couple of rental properties, and I'd like to get one of my tenants out because he's kind of a slob.

Dr. Dan: Okay, go ahead.

Caller 2: Well, the lease is up, but I know I shouldn't let him go just for that.

Dr. Dan: Why not?

Caller 2: It just doesn't seem like the most compassionate thing to do. I'm a Christian myself, and I don't think that's what Jesus would do.

Dr. Dan: You know, he might. You said your tenant was really messy, right?

Caller 2: Yeah . . .

Dr. Dan: Well, cleanliness is next to godliness, so if he's not being that clean, God must be on your side.

Caller 2: Is that in the Bible?

Dr. Dan: Oh, sure! It's in Proverbs—I think. Anyway, let your tenant go with a clear conscience.

Caller 2: Okay—thanks.

Dr. Dan: You're listening to "Nothing But the Truth" with Dr. Dan. We have an open line, and we're taking your calls. Let's go to Frank in Springfield. Frank, you're on the air.

Caller 3: Yes, Doctor. I'm calling because you always seem to give such good advice based on the scriptures.

Dr. Dan: Yes, I know. What's your question?

Caller 3: Well, my wife and I have these friends of ours over every week. We really like them and we usually have a good time . . .

Dr. Dan: So what's your question?

Caller 3: It's their kids. They're a lot more rambunctious than our kids, and we really don't feel comfortable telling them to settle down, but their parents don't think they're doing anything wrong.

Dr. Dan: Okay. Can I ask you a question?

Caller 3: Sure.

Dr. Dan: Exactly when did you have your spine removed?

Caller 3: Excuse me?

Dr. Dan: It's your house, isn't it?

Caller 3: Well, sure, but they're not my kids . . .

Dr. Dan: I don't care whose kids they are. The Bible says that kids should be seen and not heard, right?

Caller 3: It does?

Dr. Dan: Hello?!? Are you reading the same Bible I am?

Caller 3: Yeah, I guess I just didn't think that was in there.

Dr. Dan: Sure it is. I think it's in Hesitations. Give it a try. Next caller, you're on the air with Dr. Dan on Nothing But the Truth.

Caller 4: Hello, Dr. Dan?

Dr. Dan: Yes, go ahead.

Caller 4: Well, I've been listening to your show, and it seems to me that you may be spitting out some inaccuracies that your listeners may be taking as the truth.

Dr. Dan: They are truth. After all, this is Nothing But the Truth.

Caller 4: Yes, but you've been giving references to books of the Bible that don't exist for scriptures that aren't there.

Dr. Dan: I have not. You must have been listening wrong.

Caller 4: You know, that may be inaccurate as well.

Dr. Dan: Are you serious?

Caller 4: Yes, I'm serious. I think you have good intentions, but your pride may be getting in the way. And the Bible tells us, "Pride goes before destruction." So be careful, Dr. Dan.

Dr. Dan: I thought it was "pride goes before a fall", Mr. Know-it-All. And I am well aware of the dangers of being prideful. It's one of the seven deadly sins mentioned in the Old Testament.

Caller 4: Once again, that's not accurate. There's actually no mention of seven deadly sins anywhere in the Scriptures. See, you're taking worldly values and equating them to scriptural truth. You can't do that.

Dr. Dan: Sir, I think you have too much spare time on your hands! And we all know that idle hands are the devil's workshop. Now, I suppose you're going to tell me *that's* not scriptural.

Caller 4: Actually, it's not.

Dr. Dan: Well, we're nearly out of time for today. Do you have a question, or are you going to continue to refuse to believe that I know what I'm talking about?

Caller 4: If I offered anything at this point, I think it just might be casting my pearls before swine . . .

Dr. Dan: Sir, are you calling me a swine?

Caller 4: No, sir. It's from the book of Matthew. It means that I am wasting my time.

Dr. Dan: And speaking of time, we're all out. Join us next time when we screen our callers a little better. Remember, we're never wrong on Nothing But the Truth. Until next time, this is Dr. Dan, hoping all your advice is as good as mine.

Are We There Yet?

Purpose

With the challenges presented by today's society, it is very easy to allow ourselves to get stressed out. The pressures to succeed are sometimes too much to overcome. That's why it's important to develop a relationship with Christ, so that we can turn our burdens over to Him and maintain a worry-free life.

Running Time

8–10 minutes

Characters

Dad: father that has been stressed out at work and is looking for peace among his family

Mom: down-to-earth pregnant mom who is unsuccessfully trying to hold the family together

2 children: typical siblings that constantly fight among each other

Costumes

Dad: any

Mom: housedress, house shoes, wig (optional)

2 children: any

Props

4 chairs

Steering wheel

Handbag

Camera

Road map

Application

This skit is a reflection of the conventional long family vacation in the car. The dad has been stressed out at work and is beginning to take it out on his family. The better he can portray his high stress level, the better the message will be portrayed.

The role of the mom is unassuming. This skit has been very successful using a male performer to play this part, complete with the housedress, house shoes, and wig. The audience reaction alone when the performer first comes out will set the stage for the entire skit.

The two children can either be played by performers or by volunteers from the audience. Since there are no prepared lines for these characters, this can easily be done. This also presents a great chance to improvise. The children should fight among each other the entire time they are in the back seat of the car.

Scripture Reference
Hebrews 12: 14–15

[14]Make every effort to live in peace with all men and to be holy, without holiness no one will see the Lord. [15]See to it that no one misses the grace of God and that no bitter root grows up to cause trouble and defile many.

Skit
(*4 chairs are set up in two rows to portray the seats in a car; a steering wheel is under the driver's seat. Mom enters the stage holding her back, as she is pregnant; addresses the audience*)

Mom: My husband has been very stressed out at work lately, and his boss has told him that he needs to take some time off and get away. So he's decided he's going to take the family on a cross-country road trip. In the car. To the Grand Canyon. Now, he knows that I'm four months pregnant and not exactly in condition to sit in the car for long periods of time, but I'm trying to be a good wife and help him deal with his stress. Excuse me one second, but I need to sit down. (*carefully sits in the front passenger seat*) Now, I don't know what he thinks I'm going to do when I get to the Grand Canyon, but one thing is for sure, I'm not getting on one of those donkeys. And you know what he said to me? He said I better not fall down, or I might fill it up. Right now, I'm just ready to get this trip over with, if he would ever get out here. (*yelling off stage*) Honey, where are you? Would you hurry up!

Dad: I'm coming, I'm coming!

Mom: What's taking you so long?

Dad: I had to complete my honey-do list. Honey, do this; Honey, do that. (*Dad picks up the steering wheel and sits in the driver's seat.*)

Mom: Can we just get this trip over with? This was your idea, you know.

Dad: Well, it's been very stressful at work lately. My boss was always talking about how I needed to take some time off, and he kept talking about something out of Hebrews that says we should be at peace with all men. So, that's what I'm going to do on this trip, I'm going to be at peace with all men. Can we go?

Mom: I'm just going through the list in my head. Did you remember to turn off the coffeepot?

Dad: Yes, I turned off the coffeepot. Can we go?

Mom: Did you remember to cancel the newspaper?

Dad: Yes, I cancelled the newspaper. Can we go now?

Mom: Did you remember to put the hamster in the kennel?

Dad: You don't put hamsters in the kennel.

Mom: Then who's going to take care of the hamster?

Dad: I left it with the pastor. That way, if something happens to it, I know it's going to heaven.

Mom: Good thinking.

Dad: Can we go now?

Mom: There's just one thing you're forgetting.

Dad: What?

Mom: Where are your children?

Dad: Okay, fine!

(*Dad gets up and goes to get the two children, either two performers off stage or two unsuspecting people from the audience. The three come back to the stage; the two children get into the back seat and begin fighting with each other; Dad picks up the steering wheel and sits in the driver's seat.*)

Dad: There! Can we go now?

Mom: There's just one more thing. (*Dad is visibly upset; Mom gets a camera out of handbag and stands up*) I need to get a picture for the scrapbook—smile! (*snaps picture; sits back down and puts camera back in handbag*) Okay, I'm ready.

Dad: It's about time. I'm ready for a stress-free vacation.

(*several seconds pass*)

Mom: Are we there yet?

Dad: No, we're not there yet.

Mom: Well, how long is this trip going to take?

Dad: About 18 hours.

Mom: And how long have we been gone?

Dad: About 30 seconds.

Mom: Then will you tell me when we get there?

Dad: Oh, I'll tell you alright.

Mom: Thank you—are we there yet?

Dad: No, we are not there yet.

Mom: Are we there yet?

Dad: (*beginning to get annoyed*) No, we are not there yet.

Mom: Well, all I know is if you don't do something to quiet down your kids in the back seat, I'm going to go crazy.

(*Dad hands the steering wheel to Mom, who holds it while shaking. Dad then steps into the back seat and begins yelling at the kids.*)

Dad: (yelling and pointing at the kids) Listen! I'm trying to drive here! Now I want you kids to quit fighting and be quiet! I mean it! Now, don't make me come into the back seat again! (*Dad sits back down and takes the steering wheel back from Mom.*) Thank you!!

Mom: Honey, is that a vein popping out of your neck?

Dad: (*glaring at Mom*) I am at peace with all men. And he didn't say anything about women.

Mom: Are we there yet?

Dad: No, we are not there yet!

Mom: (*looking over her right shoulder behind her*) Hey, Honey! I think you missed our exit.

Dad: I know where I'm going.

Mom: No, really, I think you're lost.

Dad: I am not lost.

Mom: Don't you think you need to stop and ask for directions?

Dad: I don't need directions. I know where I'm going.

Mom: Then stop and let me ask for directions.

Dad: You don't need directions. You're not driving.

Mom: I was a minute ago. (*gets road map out of bag and struggles to unfold it*) Now, if I could just find it here.

Dad: Oh, no! Not the map! Here, give me that. (*hands Mom the steering wheel and takes the map from her*) Well, no wonder. You had the map upside down. (*flips the map around*) There. I told you I knew where we were going. (*hands the map back to Mom*)

Mom: Okay, fine—are we there yet?

Dad: No, we are not there yet.

Mom: But I need to go to the bathroom.

Dad: You've got to be kidding me. You just went.

Mom: When?

Dad: Before we left.

Mom: But that was four hours ago.

Dad: Use one of the kids' slurpee cups.

Mom: Honey, I'm serious. The baby is sitting on my bladder!

Dad: Fine! (*slams on the brakes; Mom and Dad both lean forward*) You have thirty seconds.

Mom: But it's going to take me a couple of minutes. (*Mom gets up slowly and starts walking off stage*)

Dad: Come on, hurry up. I want to stay on schedule. (*speaks to the kids*) Why don't you kids go get something to eat while we're waiting for your mom? (*kids get up and leave*)

Dad: (*once Mom and the kids are out of sight; starts to drive off*) I'm at peace with all men!

Who Is God?

Purpose

The pressure to be successful in today's society makes it easy to get caught up in the chaos of it all. It has become all too common to use the busyness of our lives as an excuse to turn from God. Sometimes, we need to look at life through the eyes of a child, as Jesus instructed us to do. It is only then we will see the importance of creating time for worship, prayer, and servanthood.

Running Time

5–7 minutes

Characters

Billy: inquisitive child, curious yet naïve in a childlike way about life around him

Tommy: child that has been raised with an understanding of who God is, although he may have a hard time verbalizing it

Costumes

Billy and Tommy: outfits that would be indicative of children, such as large, baggy clothes, caps, etc.

Props

Beach ball

Application

This skit is a reflection of the innocence of children. The more the performers can take on the personality of the children, the better off the skit will be, as the humor has the potential to be more physical than verbal. The performers should study and develop the voices and mannerisms of children. The beach ball is merely a suggested prop and can be substituted for anything that would be appropriate for the setting.

Billy is a curious young boy whose mind is racing with tons of questions. The performer will want to slow the pace and be deliberate in order to accentuate this characteristic. Billy also gets overly excited every time he figures something out.

Tommy is a more grounded individual, but is still limited in his knowledge. For the most part, he thinks he has things figured out, but you need to remember he is still a child and will have some trouble verbalizing what he wants to say. Tommy takes pride in being somewhat of a mentor for Billy.

Scripture Reference
Luke 18:16

[16]Jesus called the children to him and said, "Let the little children come to me, and do not hinder them, for the kingdom of God belongs to such as these. [17]I tell you the truth, anyone who will not receive the kingdom of God like a little child will never enter it."

Skit
(*Tommy is sitting on the floor center stage, hands folded as he is praying; Billy enters with a beach ball.*)

Billy: Hey Tommy. Whatcha doin'?

Tommy: I'm praying.

Billy: Playing what?

Tommy: Not playing. Praying.

Billy: Oh, okay. (*puzzled*) Hey Tommy, what's praying?

Tommy: It's when you talk to God about stuff.

Billy: But you weren't saying anything.

Tommy: You don't have to talk out loud. God will still hear you.

Billy: Oh—hey Tommy, I hate to break it to you, but there isn't anybody here.

Tommy: I know. My mom and dad says it's best to be alone when you pray.

Billy: But, if praying is talking to God, and there's no one here, how is He going to hear you?

Tommy: Because He's God.

Billy: Oh—who's God?

Tommy: God lives up in heaven. He made the whole world. (*spreads his arms above his head to signify the heavens*)

(*Tommy and Billy get up and start tossing the beach ball back and forth.*)

Billy: Wow. He must be strong.

Tommy: He is. One of His main jobs is making people.

Billy: You mean like babies?

Tommy: Yeah.

Billy: I thought babies came from inside their mommy's bellies.

Tommy: They do. But God makes them and puts them there.

Billy: Why doesn't He just make them be grown up? Wouldn't that be easier?

Tommy: I think babies are easier to make because they're littler. Plus, He doesn't have time to teach kids how to walk and talk and stuff. He can just leave that to the parents.

Billy: What kind of stuff do you say to God when you pray?

Tommy: Sometimes I thank Him for things.

Billy: Like what?

Tommy: Anything I can think of. I usually thank Him for my mom and my dad and my grandma and grandpa.

Billy: What else?

Tommy: Sometimes, I pray if I want something.

Billy: Cool. Can I pray?

Tommy: Yeah. Anybody can do it.

Billy: I'm going to pray for a new bike 'cause my mom and dad said I couldn't have one.

Tommy: Hey Billy, you shouldn't go over your mom and dad's head and ask for something they said you couldn't have. You'll just be wasting your time.

Billy: But I thought God wanted to help people.

Tommy: He does, but He's real busy. That's why He put parents in charge.

Billy: Hey Tommy, does God have any kids?

Tommy: Yeah, Jesus is God's Son.

Billy: Where does He go to school?

Tommy: He doesn't live on earth. But He used to. He did lots of miracles like walking on water and healing sick people.

Billy: Was He like a magician?

Tommy: Not really. He just wanted to help people. And teach people about God.

Billy: He must have been real popular.

Tommy: He was at first. But then people got tired of Him and they killed Him.

Billy: Wow. I bet that made God mad. What did He do to them?

Tommy: Nothing. See, Jesus was nice to everybody, even the people that wanted to kill Him, so He told God to forgive them. And God did.

Billy: Those people were lucky.

Tommy: Yeah, we're all lucky.

Billy: Why?

Tommy: Because three days after Jesus died, He rose from the dead. That's why we celebrate Easter.

Billy: Wow. Does that mean Jesus still lives here?

Tommy: No. After He rose from the dead, He went up to heaven so He could be with His father.

Billy: You know, when my great grandpa died, my mom said he went to heaven. But I don't think he rose from the dead.

Tommy: When regular people die, their bodies stay here, but their spirits go to heaven. But Jesus got to take His body to heaven.

Billy: What does Jesus do in heaven?

Tommy: He mostly helps His dad out, by listening to prayers and stuff.

Billy: I sometimes help my dad by cleaning my room.

Tommy: That's important, too. It's always important to do things to help you mom and dad.

Billy: I bet Jesus asks God a lot of questions.

Tommy: Not really. He pretty much knows what to do, which is good because He can take care of a lot of things without bothering God.

Billy: So he's kind of like a secretary.

Tommy: I guess, but a lot more important.

Billy: Hey Tommy, can you teach me how to pray?

Tommy: Sure. It's easy.

Billy: When is the best time to pray?

Tommy: There's really no best time.

Billy: My mom and dad usually pray before dinner. I think it's because my mom isn't a very good cook.

Tommy: You can pray any time you want.

Billy: What if God is busy?

Tommy: That's why it's good that Jesus is helping Him. I think they got it worked out so one of them is always on duty.

Billy: That makes a lot of sense—hey Tommy, where's the best place to pray?

Tommy: You can pray wherever you want. God will still hear you.

Billy: What if a lot of people are praying at the same time? How does He hear them?

Tommy: I think He figured out a way to turn the sound down in His ears.

Billy: Thanks Tommy. Hey, I think I hear my mom calling me. I better go now. You can finish praying. (*Billy walks off*)

Tommy: Thanks. (*sits back on floor*) Dear God, thank you for my mom and my dad and my grandma and grandpa. And my best friend Billy. Amen.

Anger Management

Purpose

Sometimes as Christians, we lose sight of God's instructions set forth in Scripture, and worldly pressures get the best of us, as we become quick to anger. But while we want to be sure to maintain our composure, we must also remember that it is not a sin to be angry. Jesus himself got angry several times, and in our quest to lead all to Christ, we want to maintain our enthusiasm for Him without letting anger control our emotions.

Running Time

5–7 minutes

Characters

Hank: A hillbilly that is on the lazy side and quick to get angry.

Frank: Hank's brother; he is more active.

Both Hank and Frank have interpreted the Bible in their own special way.

Costumes

Cut-off jean shorts

Muscle t-shirts

Mullet wigs

Bare feet

Props

Bible

Animal skins on a rope

Application

Hank and Frank are hillbilly brothers, so the performers can have a lot of fun developing these characters. This is another opportunity to use physical comedy to draw the audience in and then present the message.

Throughout much of this skit, the characters speak to the audience rather than to each other. This presents a good chance to interact with the audience and possibly work in some improv.

Scripture Reference
Ephesians 4:26–27

[26]In your anger do not sin. Do not let the sun go down while you are still angry, [27]and do not give the devil a foothold.

Skit
(*Hank and Frank enter from opposite ends of the stage; Frank is carrying animal skins on a rope.*)

Hank: Hey, where you been?

Frank: I got up early to go huntin'. See what I got! (*shows Hank his skins*)

Hank: What d'ya mean, you got up early to go huntin'? Why didn't you get me up?

Frank: 'Cause you hate to hunt. Besides, all you ever want to do is sleep.

Hank: Well, maybe this time I wanted to go. Ooh, this really burns me.

Frank: You're not angry, Hank, are you?

Hank: Of course not.

Frank: Good, 'cause I was afraid you were refusin' to admit you were angry.

Hank: No way, I would never deny my anger.

Frank: Do you know what we call a man that denies his anger?

Hank: No, what?

Frank: We call him a girly-man.

Hank: An angry man that denies his anger is a girly-man?

Frank: Darn tootin'. You don't want to be a girly-man, Hank, do you?

Hank: No, I certainly do not. Why does denying anger make you a girly-man, Frank?

Frank: When you deny something that everyone else knows is true, you're telling a lie.

Hank: Hey, I get it now. And when you lie, that makes you a liar.

Frank: Yeah, and when you're a liar, that makes you a girly-man. You don't want to be a girly-man, do you?

Hank: No, I want to be a manly-man. But I don't get it, Frank. How does telling a lie make you a girly-man?

Frank: (*gets a Bible*) 'Cause the Bible here says, "Be angry and sin not." That means it's not a sin to be angry.

Hank: But it is a sin to tell a lie by denying your anger? How can I do that, Frank?

Frank: Here's what you do. When you become angry, just take a second or two to remind yourself that it's not a sin to be angry.

Hank: And that'll change me from a girly-man to a manly-man? I don't believe it.

Frank: Let me give you an example. Let's suppose I stomp on

your foot. (*Frank stomps on Hank's foot.*)

Hank: (*grimaces, speaking with tension*) For example. (*gives a fake smile*)

Frank: Hank, are you angry because I'm stepping on your foot?

Hank: (*painfully*) Who, me?

Frank: (*to the audience*) Right now, because Hank is a Christian, he might think that Christians don't get angry. He might want to deny that he's angry so he'll look more spiritual to his Christian friends. Right, Hank?

Hank: (*desperate*) That's right.

Frank: Hank also takes just a second or two to remember that Jesus himself was angry several times in the Bible, but he was completely sinless. It's okay to become angry. Right, Hank?

Hank: (*desperate*) That's right.

Frank: Hank also takes time to ask the Holy Spirit to help him to "be angry and sin not."

Hank: (*desperate*) Please, Lord, help me!

Frank: Hank, you're not angry, are you?

Hank: Yes! I'm angry!

Frank: (*lifts foot; speaking to audience*) There, you see? Hank just transformed himself from a girly-man who denied his anger into a manly-man, who is not afraid to express his anger.

Hank: Hey Frank, I really feel better now. What else have you learned in that there Bible of yours?

Frank: I learned that a lot of them disciples were fishermen, like Simon and Andrew.

Hank: That's pretty cool, 'cause I like to fish, too. I wonder what kind of bait they used.

Frank: I don't know. Hey, you think Noah woulda made a good fisherman?

Hank: I doubt it. You can't do much with only two worms.

Frank: You got a good point. You got a favorite Scripture, Hank?

Hank: Actually, I do. (*takes Bible from Frank*) I like singing, and there's a bunch of parts of the Bible that talks about music. Like Psalm 150, that says we should "praise him with tambourine and dancing, and praise him with strings and flute."

Frank: It sounds to me like God likes country music.

Hank: I think you're right. I'm pretty sure there were fiddles in there somewhere.

Frank: Hey, since you like to sing, why don't you give us something?

Hank: Okay. (*singing*) "As the deer panteth o'er the water, I shot him with my 44".

Frank: Hank, that's terrible!

Hank: Hold on, I got another one. (*singing*) "Ford, I lift your name on high. You're much better than a Chevy . . ."

Frank: Is that the best you can do?

Hank: What are you talking about? I'm just having some fun.

Frank: Look, Hank! I'm not going to let you disrespect God like that!

Hank: Settle down, Frank. If I didn't know any better, I'd say you were blowing off steam without giving it a second thought.

Frank: What's wrong with someone who blows off steam without giving it a second thought?

Hank: We call him a girly-man.

Frank: Someone who blows off steam without giving it a second thought is a girly-man?

Hank: That's right. But I can help you. Do you know how to become a manly-man when you get angry?

Frank: I'm going to take a stab at this one. I'll bet you don't blow off steam without giving it a second thought.

Hank: That's right. A manly-man will take just a second or two to think about his anger.

Frank: Just a second or two? That's all it takes to be a manly-man?

Hank: Yeah, during the first second or two after you become angry, you reject the idea that just blowing off steam is the way to vent your anger.

Frank: Hey, I think I understand now. Blowing off steam is for girly-men.

Hank: Yeah, but the manly-man will say to himself, "What's the best way to express my anger that won't hurt people?"

Frank: A manly-man doesn't want to hurt people. People who hurt people are weak and puny.

Hank: And you don't want to be weak and puny. You want to be a manly-man, right, Frank?

Frank: How do you know?

Hank: (*gets Bible*) It says right here in the Bible that "Everyone should be quick to listen, slow to speak and *slow* to become angry." Let me give you an example. (*Hank stomps on Frank's foot.*) Suppose I stomp on Frank's foot.

Frank: (*grimaces, speaking with tension*) For example. (*gives a fake smile*)

Hank: (*speaking to audience*) Right now, Frank would just love to punch my lights out, wouldn't you, Frank?

Frank: You bet. (*pastes on smile*)

Hank: But instead, Frank pauses for just a second or two in order to think about the most appropriate way to express his anger.

Frank: (*painfully*) Gee, I wonder how I could express my anger appropriately!

Hank: This also gives Frank time to include the Holy Spirit.

Frank: (*desperately*) Holy Spirit!

Hank: Now, with the help of the Holy Spirit, Frank comes up with the most appropriate way to express his anger.

Frank: (*desperately*) Hank, could you please remove your foot?

Hank: Yeah, sure. (*lifts foot*) See, Frank, that's what it takes to turn yourself from a girly-man to a manly-man.

Frank: Y'know, I do feel pretty good.

Hank: You ready for another song?

Frank: No way do I want you singing again.

Hank: Alright then, Smarty Pants, you're so great, you try singing.

Frank: Now Hank, you know I don't sing—but I like telling jokes. You know, God's got a pretty good sense of humor.

Hank: This oughta be good.

Frank: Knock knock.

Hank: Nice try. He's God, so He already knows who's there.

Frank: Okay, fine. Let me try another one. Three men walk into a bar.

Hank: God's already heard this one. He doesn't think it's very funny.

Frank: That's it! Get out!

Hank: What's wrong, Frank? Are you getting angry? (*Hank exits*)

Frank: Yes, I'm angry! And you know why? Because it's okay to be angry! (*to audience*) Now where was I? Oh yeah, let me finish that joke I started before I was so rudely interrupted. Three men walk into a bar, and the fourth one ducked. You get it? See, when I said three men walk into a bar, most people would think I'm talking about a drinking establishment. But what I was really talkin' about was the kind of bar that's long and made out of metal, so when he ran into it, they hurt themselves. That's why the fourth one ducked, 'cause he saw the other ones get hurt and he didn't want to get hurt, too— well, I think I get the picture. I can see you people aren't going to get any better. Boy, this burns me! Let me go find Hank. (*Frank exits*)

Are You Too Busy?

Purpose

It has become too easy to get caught up in earthly rewards as we struggle to be "perfect." We rush around, doing whatever it takes to become successful. The problem is, our idea of success has become distorted because it does not include Christ. Even when our intentions are good, it is important that we take the time to develop a relationship and spend time with Him through prayer. Christ requires our best efforts, and when those efforts are put forth to strengthen God's kingdom, then the Lord will be pleased in our work.

Running Time

5–7 minutes

Characters

Martha: a compulsive grandmother who is obsessed with making everything perfect.

Props

Long scroll of paper
Any number household cleaning items

Costumes

House dress
Apron

Application

This is a 1-woman skit that examines the pressures we place on ourselves to make things perfect. In this skit, you have the option of using a varied number of props, but the message gets across well if the performer is able to act out the different chores with little or no props. A comical costume helps add to the physical humor. The performer should be frantic and rushed in order to present the message.

This skit also gives the performer a great opportunity to improvise. The script and the suggested props are given merely as a guide. Use different parts of the stage to represent different rooms or areas of the house. Interact with the audience where possible.

Scripture Reference
Luke 10:38–42

[38]As Jesus and his disciples were on their way, he came to a village where a woman named Martha opened her home to him. [39]She had a sister called Mary, who sat at the Lord's feet listening to what he said. [40]But Martha was distracted by all the preparations that had to be made. She came to him and asked, "Lord, don't you care that my sister has left me to do the work by myself? Tell her to help me!" [41]"Martha, Martha," the Lord answered, "you are worried and upset about many things, [42]but only one thing is needed. Mary has chosen what is better, and it will not be taken away from her.

Skit
(*If possible, this skit works well if Martha is able to enter the stage through the audience, talking to herself and interacting with the audience as she approaches the stage.*)

Martha: Oh, let's see, the kids will be here in an hour. There's no way I'll have everything ready before they get here. (*looks in the oven*) Oh, good. The turkey's almost done. Good thing, because if I don't get this ham in soon it will never get done on time. Now let me look over this menu and see if there's anything I forgot. (*rolls out long piece of paper*) Turkey, ham, mashed potatoes, sweet potatoes. (*looks up*) Oh, no! I forgot to get the sweet potatoes on. Justin will be so upset if I don't make the sweet potatoes. Let me get the water boiling while I peel some real quick. (*peels potatoes while holding the list under her arm; continues to read*) Let's see, what else do I need? Peas, beets, (*looks up again*) The beets! You know how Keith has to have his beets done just right so he can dip his ham in the beet juice! (*looks at the stove*) When am I going to get to the beets? Every eye on the stove is being used right now! Let's see . . . potatoes, sweet potatoes, peas, corn . . . it looks like the peas will be done first. Then I can throw the beets on there, and they should be done just in time. (*hesitates for a moment*) Okay, where was I? (*looks at the menu again*) Dinner rolls are right here. They go in the oven last so they'll be warm when we sit down to eat. (*frantically*) Cranberries! I forgot to put the cranberries in the refrigerator! Oh, the kids are going to kill me. I forgot the cranberries last time they were here. Maybe if I put them in the freezer, they'll be cold by the time we sit down to eat.

(*Martha takes off her apron and moves to a different part of the stage.*) I've gotta let dinner alone for about 10 minutes while I straighten up in the living room. (*rushing around*) My goodness, I haven't vacuumed all day! Look at this floor. Let me get the carpet swept. (*begins vacuuming*) Okay, now I need to make sure the nap is all going the same direction. The kids would never forgive me if they saw this carpet with the nap going every which way. Besides, by having the nap all going the same direction, if somebody ever broke into the house in the middle of the night and tried to rob me, you'd be able to tell exactly where they went because the nap would be all messed up. See, sometimes my kids don't understand why I do things, but there's a perfectly good reason for everything I do. There, that looks good. Oh, look, there are spots on the coffee table. Let me get the Pledge so I can polish this furniture real quick. (*polishes tables; takes a deep breath as she looks at her reflection*) Ah, beautiful! I'm glad I got these curtains washed earlier this week. I never would have had time to do it today. Oh no! There are fingerprints on the TV! Let me wipe those off. You know, if anybody saw the way this house looks right now, they would think I was the worst mother in the world.

(*Martha finishes dusting and sits down for a moment; takes a deep breath*) The kids will be here any minute. Let me sit here for two seconds to catch my breath before I finish getting dinner ready. (*looks at herself*) Oh, look at me! I can't be seen with this on when they get here. Let me go find a good dress to put on. (*moves to a different part of the stage; rummages through hanging clothes in the closet*) Let's see, my green dress with white flowers would be perfect. Where in the world is it? Oh, I bet it's still dirty. I knew I should have stayed up to do that extra load of laundry last night. Here, let me get this laundry started. (*struggles to carry heavy load of laundry to a different part of the stage*) It'll never be done before they get here, but there's nothing else I can do right now. This is so embarrassing. Now, back to what I'll wear for the kids. I have this yellow outfit, but I wore that last time they visited. They're going to think it's the only thing I own, but it's the only thing I have that doesn't make me look like a bum. (*sits down, disgusted*) Nothing is working out right! I wanted everything to be just perfect, but it's all falling apart. What am I going to do?

(*Phone rings. Martha answers phone*) Hello . . . Hi, Janice, what are you doing today? . . . Oh, no, I'd love to go to church with you today, but I can't. The kids are coming in today, and I don't have a single thing ready . . . I know I should probably go to church more often, but I just don't have time . . . The last time I went? I don't know, probably Easter. Besides, I don't have to go to church to be a good person. I do plenty of good things without going to church . . . But nothing is ready. If I leave now, the kids will be coming in to a messy house. I could never do that to them. And dinner isn't anywhere near ready . . . I'm not exaggerating. You know how much of a neat freak Keith is . . . Well, even if he did get it from me, I'd hate to disappoint him. And I certainly don't have time to go to church . . . By the time they get here, they would have been on the road all morning. I'm sure they'll just want to come in and get something to eat. They're not going to be interested in going to church. They never go to church . . . Okay, so they go to church, but have you ever seen the way that Lori keeps that house of theirs? Maybe if she stayed home once in a while . . . No, I know everything will still be here when I get back . . . But I don't have anything to wear to church . . . I know these kids wear whatever they want to church these days, but I couldn't disrespect the church that way . . . Okay, if you're sure. I'll meet you at church as soon as the kids get here. (*hangs up phone*) I don't quite understand it, but I guess I'll go as I am. Let me go watch for the kids. (*walks off stage*).

That'll Leave a Mark

Purpose

True success in life can only be achieved through a strong relationship with Christ. The pressures of society put too much emphasis on wealth and power, but these things are not of God. Earthly possessions have no spiritual value; the only true treasures are those found in heaven.

Running Time

8–10 minutes

Characters

J.T. McAllister: a wealthy southern CEO of a major corporation who values status and material wealth

Barbie: J.T.'s young, attractive, ditzy secretary

Helen: J.T.'s wife, a dedicated Christian who prefers a simple life

Johnson: J.T.'s bumbling assistant manager

Costumes

J.T. McAllister: business suit, cowboy hat

Barbie: any

Helen: modest outfit

Johnson: shirt and tie / business casual

Props

Desk

Chair

Telephone

Application

This skit takes place in the office of J.T. McAllister, an arrogant, wealthy businessman. Each of the characters in this skit has a distinct personality, and these characteristics should be enhanced to reveal the message.

J.T. is convinced that he has achieved all of his success on his own, without God's help. It is important that his self-value be overstated, because in spite of all of his success, his life is falling apart around him. While God keeps sending messages his way, J.T. is blind to them until it is too late.

Barbie is a stereotypical secretary, young and "blonde" in nature. While she lacks common sense, she is faithful to God. She resists J.T.'s charm and flirtations.

Helen is a faithful wife, but she is a more faithful Christian, as her values differ greatly from J.T.'s. This closeness to God has led to her simple life, and she holds firm to those values as she refuses to compromise her beliefs for J.T.'s riches.

Johnson is the ultimate "yes man." While he is as strong in his faith as Barbie and Helen, He lacks self-confidence. He also doesn't have the relationship with Christ needed to stand up for his values.

Scripture Reference

1 John 2:15–17

[15]Do not love the world or anything in the world. If anyone loves the world, the love of the Father is not in him. [16]For everything in the world—the cravings of sinful man, the lust of his eyes and the boasting of what he has and does—comes not from the Father but from the world. [17]The world and its desires pass

away, but the man who does the will of God lives forever.

Skit

(*The scene begins with J.T. sitting behind his desk.*)

J.T.: (*picks up the phone*) Barbie, could you come in here, please.

(*Barbie enters*)

Barbie: Yes, Mr. McAllister.

J.T.: Barbie, I was just going over these letters you typed today, and I noticed a couple of mistakes.

Barbie: Really? But I was so careful. What did I do wrong?

J.T.: Well, nothing that bad, really. It's just that this letter to General Motors should not begin "Dear General."

Barbie: Well, you know, I was just trying to be polite, Mr. McAllister.

J.T.: You've got a good point, Barbie, and I can appreciate that. But General Motors is not a real person. It's a corporation — a company — (*Barbie has a blank look on her face*) never mind. Besides, I wouldn't want you to break a fingernail from working too hard. I'll just send these letters to the secretarial pool to have them typed.

Barbie: Wow, Mr. McAllister! I didn't know there's a pool for secretaries! I'll bring my swimsuit tomorrow.

J.T.: No, I mean . . . Oh, never mind. Why don't you go ahead and bring your swimsuit. (*makes a pass*) It will improve the scenery around here.

Barbie: (*slaps J.T.*) Mr. McAllister! You're a married man.

J.T.: What the old bag doesn't know won't hurt her.

Barbie: Mr. McAllister, you shouldn't be so mean to your wife. She loves you very much.

J.T.: Look, I've been married for 25 years. Don't I deserve a little fun once in a while?

Barbie: Not like this, you don't. You know, adultery is a sin according to the Ten Commandments.

J.T.: And insubordination is a sin according to the Board of Directors.

Barbie: Mr. McAllister, I answer to a higher authority than your Board of Directors.

J.T.: You know, I never figured you to be the religious type.

Barbie: That's the way I was raised, Mr. McAllister.

J.T.: Stop calling me Mr. McAllister. Call me J.T. All of my friends do.

Barbie: Thank you, J.T.

J.T.: By the way, it's getting late and I've got a ton of work to do. I don't suppose you could stay and help me?

Barbie: Sorry, Mr. McAllister, uh, I mean J.T. But I've got something I need to do tonight.

J.T.: Really, what's that?

Barbie: If you must know, I've got to baby-sit my nephew tonight.

J.T.: Well, of course you do. You just run along, Barbie. I'll get somebody else to help me tonight.

(*Barbie exits; J.T. picks up the phone*)

J.T.: Johnson! I need you in here right away.

(*Johnson rushes in*)

Johnson: Yes, J.T., ol' buddy. (*puts his arm around J.T.'s shoulder*)

J.T.: Mere middle managers do not call corporate presidents by their first names. This is a professional company. (*pushes Johnson away*) And get away from me!

Johnson: Yes, J.T., I mean Mr. McAllister, I just thought . . .

J.T.: Now, there you go again. When I'm interested in your opinion, I'll give it to you. Now, let's get down to business. Do you have any news on our takeover attempt of Olive Oil?

Johnson: No, J.T., I mean Mr. McAllister, they're still in executive session. Uh, by the way, I heard there's going to be an opening now that old man Byrd is retiring. You know, you're going to need a VP to replace him, and I was thinking that, with my hard work and experience, I would be available should you decide to . . .

J.T.: You? A vice president? Oh, believe me, Johnson, if the subject ever comes up, you'll get all the consideration you deserve.

Johnson: (*vigorously shaking hands with J.T.*) Oh, thank you, Sir.

J.T.:   Cut that out! (*pushes Johnson away*) Hey, by the way, I need somebody to stay late to help me with a project tonight. It would give me a chance to see you in action.

Johnson: I'd love to, Mr. McAllister, but my daughter's getting married tonight. There are over 200 people coming. She's so excited.

J.T.:   Really! Now, Johnson, if you're ever going to make it to VP, you need to get your priorities in order. You can't let your family life interfere with your career.

Johnson: But, Mr. McAllister, Marie is my only daughter. This will be the only chance I'll get to walk her down the aisle.

J.T.:   Doesn't she have an uncle or someone who could do it?

Johnson: Actually, she has three uncles. But that's not the point. This is a special time between a father and daughter that only happens once.

J.T.:   Nonsense! In these days and times, nobody gets married just once. You can give her away the next time.

Johnson: Next time? Marriage is a sacred vow taken before God. Making a lifetime commitment with your spouse is something that my family happens to take very seriously.

J.T.:   Listen, Johnson, your first commitment needs to be your job. Don't you want to provide your family with all the best things in life?

Johnson: J.T., I mean Mr. McAllister, the best thing I can give my family is me. The Bible teaches that we should not value earthly possessions.

J.T.:   Now don't you start that preaching thing you like to do. There's work to be done.

Johnson: Right, Sir. I don't know what I was thinking. I'll call my wife right now and tell her they'll have to start without me.

J.T.:   That's more like it. I'll call you when I'm ready for you.

Johnson: Glad to help.

(*Johnson exits; phone rings*)

J.T.:   Hello, McAllister here . . . Oh, it's you, Dear. Where are you? . . . What do you mean, you're here? I've told you to never come to my office during the day! Whatever you do, don't come prancing through the building.

(*J.T. hangs up the phone, Helen enters*)

Helen: Hello, Dear.

J.T.:   Helen, what are you doing here?

Helen: I wanted to show you the gift I picked out for the wedding.

J.T.:   Are you still going on about that wedding? That's all you've been able to talk about. Besides, look at you. You're not planning on going out looking like that, are you?

Helen: I'm sorry, J.T. I know how much you're ashamed of me.

J.T.:   That's not it, exactly. You know what the problem is? You refuse to act and dress the way a rich man's wife should.

We've got to impress people with our wealth and power so we can intimidate them. Do you think you can handle that?

Helen: I thought I dressed okay. When we were first married, you used to always tell me how attractive I was.

J.T.: It's not you, Helen, it's your clothes. And it's not even that they're that bad really, they're just so—middle class. I want my wife to dazzle with big diamonds and furs and light up the town in $2,000 dresses. Quite frankly, I'm embarrassed to have you around my friends.

Helen: Actually, Dear, I made this dress myself.

J.T.: You made it? How could you? Promise you won't mention this to anybody. How embarrassing!

Helen: But I like sewing and cooking and doing things for my family. I need to have something to keep me busy since you're always working late. When was the last time you talked to any of our children?

J.T.: I write to, uh—which one is in school? Oh, yeah—Jason, I write to Jason all the time.

Helen: Really? And just what do you write?

J.T.: A check. I send him his tuition for medical school every semester.

Helen: He's not in medical school, he's in law school! You don't even know what your own children are doing. You know, things are a lot worse than I thought. I think we need to see a counselor.

J.T.:   Me, see a shrink? No way! People who need to cry on someone else's shoulder are nothing but a bunch of stupid, spineless bores.

(*Johnson rushes in*)

Johnson: Did you call, sir? Oh, I'm sorry, I didn't realize you had somebody with you.

J.T.:   Oh, this is my—uh—cleaning lady. (*to Helen*) Look at these windows! If you want to keep this job, you've got to do better than this.

Johnson: Sir, let me be the first to congratulate you. You are now controlling stockholder and chairman of the board of Olive Oil.

J.T.:   Well, what do you know, I pulled it off.

Johnson: Just think, J.T., I mean Mr. McAllister, your name will become a household word. From now on, whenever people talk about high gas prices, they'll mention your name.

J.T.:   Do you really think so?

Johnson: Sure, you will be to gas what McDonald's is to fine dining.

J.T.:   Well, Johnson, what are you standing around for? You have work to do.

Johnson: Actually, Mr. McAllister, I was wondering, in light of this good news, if you would mind if I left now. I could still make it to the reception.

J.T.: Oh, what the heck, go on. But don't stay out too late. We have a busy day tomorrow.

Johnson: (*vigorously shakes J.T.'s hand*) Yes, sir. Thank you, sir.

(*Johnson exits*)

J.T.: Honey, isn't this exciting? This oil deal will make us rich. Filthy rich.

Helen: That doesn't matter to me.

J.T.: I'm talking Bill Gates rich.

Helen: There's only one thing I want.

J.T.: The Hope Diamond? No problem.

Helen: No, J.T., I'm not talking about . . .

J.T.: The Taj Mahal? The Eiffel Tower? You name it, it's yours.

Helen: No, you're missing the point. I would gladly give up everything if you would just become a Christian.

J.T.: Look, Helen, we've been over this a thousand times. I don't need God. After all, I built my business empire myself, without God's help.

Helen: J.T., I'm really worried about you.

J.T.: I'll tell you what, Helen, I'll make a deal with you. Stop going to that little country church on the corner and join the First United Downtown Church and I will go with you at least once a month.

Helen: Why them?

J.T.:   Because they're huge. Do you have any idea how much they paid for those stained glass windows they have? And all of the biggest politicians and businessmen go there. Think of the contacts I could make.

Helen: Sorry, J.T., I can't do it.

J.T.:   Why not? What difference does it make what church you go to?

Helen: I can't go to a church that doesn't honor Christ.

J.T.:   And I won't go to a church that doesn't honor the governor. Now, I've got a ton of work to do, Helen. What's it going to be?

Helen: J.T., don't do this to me. We've got too many years together to let it come to this.

J.T.:   Come to what? Why don't you just go home and fix me something to eat, and I'll see you as soon as I'm done here.

Helen: I'm serious, J.T., things have got to change, or I'm leaving you.

J.T.:   I don't have time for this, Helen. Now go on home, and we'll forget we ever had this discussion.

Helen: That's it. It's been nice knowing you. Goodbye, J.T.

(*Helen exits*)

J.T.: OW! (*J.T. holds his forehead as if he just got hit on the head; realizes the Helen has left him for good*) Wait a minute, Helen! Where are you going? Do you think we could talk about this? It's not as bad as it seems. Helen!

(*J.T. exits, following Helen*)

Something to Say

Purpose

We all know somebody, a close friend or relative, who enjoys hearing him or herself talk. He or she might be a self-declared expert on all things and has the ability to ramble on endlessly, not really saying anything in particular. Scripture tells us that we are to pray without ceasing, and we should only speak those words which will glorify God and His Kingdom.

Running Time

5–7 minutes

Characters

Paul: an average person
Ray: Paul's brother; he doesn't know when to stop talking.

Costumes

Paul and Ray: any

Props

None

Application

This scene is a meeting between two brothers that haven't seen each other recently, so this is a chance to catch up. Ray is a fast-talker and an expert about everything. The more long-winded and boring Ray can be, the more successful the skit will be. If not, you won't be able to end the skit fast enough for the audience. This will also make the message that much more effective.

This script should be used as a guide only. Use this as an opportunity to work in some stories about local events. This can also be used as an improv piece. The performers can use this as an opportunity to cross each other up, which goes over well in live performance.

Scripture Reference
Romans 8:26–27

26The Spirit helps us in our weakness. We do not know what we ought to pray for, but the Spirit himself intercedes for us with groans that words cannot express. 27And he who searches our hearts knows the mind of the Spirit, because the Spirit intercedes for the saints in accordance with God's will.

Skit
(*The skit opens with Paul at center stage. He recognizes Ray walking to the stage from the back, if the venue allows for that, and enthusiastically greets him.*)

Paul: Hey, Ray! I sure am glad you could make it into town. Dinner will be ready in a few minutes. How has my baby brother been?

Ray: Well, Paul, I can't complain. I just got in from the airport. Boy, was that a rough flight. I've never had such a rough flight from San Francisco to here. Now, there was that one time I was flying from San Francisco to Houston. That was a rough flight. We hit some really bad turbulence; I'm guessing it was around New Mexico. Or was it Arizona. No, I was right the first time, it was New Mexico. For a minute I didn't think we were going to make it. This lady sitting next to me was really starting to panic. Man, she was making me nervous. She grabbed onto my arm and wouldn't let go. I said "Lady, let go of my arm!" She wouldn't listen to me. But then the stewardess brought her this medicine. I think it was some kind of sedative because it knocked her out until we got to Houston. You ever been to Houston, Paul? I tell ya, that has got to be the hottest city I've ever been in. You know why? Because it's not just hot, it's humid. I don't know how people live there. I always liked living here.

Paul: Yeah, me too. So, Ray, what are you going to do while you're in town?

Ray: I've got some people I want to look up while I'm here. You remember Darrell Taylor? I haven't seen him for years. You should have seen him in high school. He was the big shot starting quarterback. I remember the game against St. John's our senior season. We had a chance to win the league championship. It was freezing rain and snow, and the field was a mud pit. It was so bad that by the end of the game you couldn't tell one team from the other. I remember he ran this quarterback draw that fooled everybody to win the game. Anyhow, I hear Darrell has become this big shot investment banker. I would have never believed in high school that he would have made anything of himself. He was such a goof off in school. Hey, didn't you go to school with Darrell's older sister? What was her name?

Paul: Becky. Her name was Becky. And yes, she was in my class.

Ray: That's right! Becky Taylor! Except she's not Taylor now. I can't remember what that guy's name is that she married. I remember her from when you guys were seniors. She was a really good swimmer, wasn't she? I remember she qualified for the Olympic trials that year. That would have been something, wouldn't it, to think somebody from our school almost made the Olympics. You know, I always like watching the Olympics. My favorite sport to watch is the one where they ride the horses. You know, I liked the Olympics better when there weren't all these professional athletes in it. But the thing about it, all those Eastern block countries all really had professionals anyhow. Especially the East German women swimmers. Man, they were buff. Didn't they finally admit that they were taking steroids? I bet it took a real genius to figure that one out. And what's with all these new sports that they keep adding to the Olympics? Did you ever notice how America seems to always do well in the sports we invented? When are they going to start taking some things away, like yachting or fencing? And since when is putting up a fence a sport?

Paul: Fencing is not putting up a fence. It'd dueling, like sword fighting.

Ray: Oh yeah! It's like medieval days, right? Did I ever tell you we took the kids to the Renaissance Festival last year? I had never been there before. Everybody there was dressed in these wild old-time costumes, and they were acting out those sword fights and there were musicians and people doing magic and all kinds of stuff. I got autographs from the Knights who say "Nee." The kids liked the magic the best. Now the food was the only thing that wasn't mostly like from Renaissance times. There were some places that were cooking this gross stuff over an open fire, and that was cool to watch them do that. I was afraid to try any of that stuff. They still had food stands all over the place like you were at the

State Fair. Somehow I don't think they ate pizza and elephant ears back in the old days. Well, maybe elephant ears, but they weren't the sugary kind. Now the State Fair, there's the best value in town. Except I don't like the rides. The kids like them, but I don't trust any amusement ride that isn't bolted down and permanent, like at King's Island or Cedar Point.

Paul: Come on Ray, we're getting ready to sit down to dinner. You get your usual spot at the table.

Ray: You know, that's one of the things I like about coming home. Some things never change. Everybody has their own spot at the table. I remember when I had to sit at the kids table. I was like 18, and I wanted to be at the adult table so bad, but I had to be the oldest person at the kids table. And Thanksgiving dinner starts at 3:00 sharp. Same as always. And smell that food. Mmmm! I think Sheri did a wonderful job, as always. Now let me look at that turkey to make sure it's not too dry. Hey Sheri, you know what the key is to keeping a turkey moist? Baste it with its own juices. Did you make your homemade gravy like you do every year? You know how much I like your homemade gravy. And I hope you didn't make the potatoes too lumpy. You know I don't like lumps in my potatoes. Let's see, oh good, you remembered the cranberries. You remember that year you forgot to put the cranberries in the refrigerator, so at the last minute you put them in the freezer to try to save them. What a disaster! I did not envy you that day.

Paul: Okay, Ray, it looks like everybody is at the table. Would you have the honor of blessing our meal for us?

Ray: What? Me, pray? But I can't think of a thing to say.

The Temple of God

Purpose
Maintaining good health is an integral part of living a Christian life. We are taught the importance of giving of our time and our resources for the glory of God. But we sometimes forget to take care of ourselves. We must remember that our bodies are strictly vessels given to us by God to take care of while we're here on earth. We study the Word to prepare our minds for Him; let's also develop a healthy diet and exercise plan to prepare our bodies for God's glory.

Running Time
5–7 minutes

Characters
Oscar: An overweight, lazy slob
Kenny: An energetic self-starter that likes to work out.

Costumes
Oscar: Jeans, tight t-shirt
Kenny: Workout clothes

Props
Bag of chips
Container of chip dip
Bag of Oreo cookies
2-liter bottle of diet pop
Remote control
TV Guide

Bible
Chair

Application

The goal of this skit is to get the audience to reflect on their shortcomings when it comes to taking care of their bodies. The success hinges on the role of Oscar. The more the performer is willing to do to overstate the fact that he's an overweight slob (such as pulling his t-shirt up to expose his belly), the more successful the physical comedy will be.

In contrast, the role of Kenny is understated. The more this performer can be active and energetic, the more the audience will see Oscar's shortcomings.

Scripture Reference

1 Corinthians 6:19–20

[19]Do you not know that your body is a temple of the Holy Spirit, who is in you, whom you have received from God? You are not your own; [20]you were bought at a price. Therefore honor God with your body.

Skit

(*The skit opens with Oscar sitting in a chair at center stage with a bag of chips, chip dip, a bag of cookies, remote control and TV Guide by his side. A 2-liter bottle of pop and a Bible are set off to the side. Kenny enters from behind Oscar.*)

Kenny: (*Clears his throat*)

Oscar: (*Stuffing his face with chips*) Oh, hey Kenny. (*offers him some chips*) Want some chips?

Kenny: No, get those things away from me.

Oscar: I'm sorry, where are my manners? (*offers him some dip*) You can't have chips without dip.

Kenny: No thank you. Everything you have here is nothing but grease and fat.

Oscar: What's your point?

Kenny: Don't you have any granola? Or fruit?

Oscar: (*looking through his things, grabs the bag of cookies*) I have some Double-Stuff Oreos.

Kenny: Man, do you realize what your arteries must look like? You're going to be dead in ten years if you don't start eating right.

Oscar: You know what I say; what's the use of living a long life if you're going to be miserable doing it?

Kenny: It doesn't have to be miserable. Look, the reason I came over was to see if you wanted to go to the park with me and the boys.

Oscar: Huh? What for?

Kenny: We were going to get a game of football going.

Oscar: Kenny, why work up a sweat when you have a whole day of games on TV? (*channel surfing with the remote control*) What do we have, ABC, CBS, 4 or 5 ESPNs?

Kenny: But it's such a beautiful day outside.

Oscar: Then open up the shades. We can admire the beauty from here.

Kenny: No, I mean let's go outside and do something.

Oscar: Isn't it too cold outside today? Or is it too hot? Man, I can't even remember what month it is. The fact is, I keep it a perfect 72 degrees in here, all the time, no wind or rain or snow. See, no need to go outside.

Kenny: But it's a perfect chance to get outside and get some exercise.

Oscar: Let me demonstrate. (*gets up and walks across the stage, picks up the 2-liter bottle of pop and returns to his chair*) I get all the exercise I need right here, walking from the living room to the kitchen and back to the living room. And I do that several times a day.

Kenny: Ooh, all in one day?

Oscar: Wait, that's not all. When a double commercial comes on the TV, you know, the 4-minute ones, I go all the way upstairs to the bathroom.

Kenny: Wow! Stairs too! I love the motivation.

Oscar: Thanks. My key is pacing myself throughout the day.

Kenny: I'll tell you what. Since you don't want to go outside, how about coming to the gym with me?

Oscar: But I get all the workout I need here with my 2-liter curls. (*curls 2-liter bottle*)

Kenny: That's 2 liters of nothing but sugar and caffeine.

Oscar: But it's diet. (*points to label on bottle*)

Kenny: And that makes it alright?

Oscar: You know, Kenny, you sure have been riding me a lot lately. What gives?

Kenny: You don't know this, but back before we met, I was actually bigger than you are now. But I got on a diet and exercise program.

Oscar: Look, I've tried every diet out there. None of them work.

Kenny: You're right; diet and exercise alone don't work. But I found something in this book that not only was crucial to my success, but it also gave me a whale of a workout. In fact, I'll bet you have this book right here in your house. Where do you keep your books?

Oscar: There's a bookcase over there. (*points to the side of the stage*)

Kenny: (*walks to the side of the stage, gets the Bible*) Let's see—here we go. This is what I'm looking for. (*walks back to Oscar*) Oscar, this here is the best workout book I've ever read.

Oscar: Hang on; let me put my stuff down. (*puts everything on the floor*) Whatcha got?

Kenny: Here you go. The Bible will bulk you up in no time.

Oscar: Geez, that book looks pretty big. I'll bet its heavy, too. You know what they say, when you first start out with a new program, you should start small and work your way up. (*picks up TV Guide*) I think my TV Guide is more my size.

Kenny: Oscar, I'm serious. I really want to see you eating better.

Oscar: But I'm the best eater I know.

Kenny: Have you ever even opened a Bible?

Oscar: I—uh . . .

Kenny: Let me rephrase that. That would have required physical work. Have you ever read anything in the Bible?

Oscar: Well, you know, I'm very busy right now, and I really don't have time for . . .

Kenny: I think I get the picture. So I'm going to help you out. I'm going to share with you a passage from 1 Corinthians, which says, "Do you not know that your body is a temple of the Holy Spirit, who is in you, whom you have received from God?"

Oscar: My body, a temple?

Kenny: Yeah.

Oscar: Look, I can believe that of someone like you. But look at me.

Kenny: That's the beauty of Scripture, Oscar. It applies to everyone.

Oscar: (*stands up and thinks about what Kenny said*) Wow, my body a temple. I kind of like that. (*puffs out chest; looks out beyond the audience*) Then I shall have the grandest temple in all the land!

Kenny: You know, I don't think it's exactly what the Lord had in mind, but it's a start. (*Kenny and Oscar walk off stage together*) Now wouldn't your temple look beautiful out in the sunlight?

You Can't Do Everything

Purpose

God has given each of us talents and abilities, and it is our responsibility to determine what those abilities are. Once we make the decision to utilize our talents for the glory of God, they then become gifts. It is not acceptable to just sit back and wait for something to happen. There are a number of different ways in which to serve Him, and we need to roll up our sleeves, get dirty, and let God reveal our gifts to us.

Running Time

12–15 minutes

Characters

Minister: A traditional southern preacher with very little patience.

Mike: An average guy who just wants to help out in church, despite the fact that he hasn't figured out what his gifts are.

Costumes

Minister: suit and tie

Mike: Any

Props

Bible

Guitar

Paper plate

Bulletin

Cap

Sunglasses

Application

This skit is an examination of our gifts, or lack thereof. The goal is to get the audience to reflect on their own gifts, and this is done by highlighting the lack of one individual's gifts. The skit takes place in a typical worship service, and it quickly goes through some of the standard components of a service. Some of the elements, such as the announcements, can easily be changed to fit the local venue.

Mike is an average guy who sincerely wants to help out during the service. The more enthusiastic he can be about helping out, the better. There are no limitations to this character. There are many chances to interact with the audience, which also lends itself to some great opportunities to improvise. One of the keys to this skit is highlighting the lack of talent in this character, so the more outrageous he can be, the better.

By contrast, the more understated the minister can be, the more impact it will have on the overall message. With each passing moment, the minister gets more and more irritated with the foolishness of Mike. Deep down, he knows Mike means well, but all he can think about is how much the service is failing. Facial expressions and actions carry as much weight as the spoken word for this character.

Scripture Reference
Romans 12:6–8

6We all have different gifts, according to the grace given us. If a man's gift is prophesying, let him use it in proportion to his faith. 7If it is serving, let him serve; if it is teaching, let him teach; 8if it is encouraging, let him encourage; if it is contributing to the needs of others, let him give generously; if it is leadership, let him govern diligently; if it is showing mercy, let him do it cheerfully.

Skit
(*The Minister enters the stage and goes to the lectern. He addresses the congregation to begin a Sunday morning service.*)

Minister: Praise the Lord, Brothers and Sisters, and welcome today to the Church of Wayward Saints of the Almighty God. We're gathered here today in the name of our Lord, Jesus Christ, to be Holy as God is Holy . . .

(*Mike enters from the back of the room, being loud and disruptive as he looks for a seat.*)

Mike: Excuse me, excuse me. Man, I tell you, you show up late for church and you can't find a place to sit. (*finding an empty spot, he speaks to the person sitting next to him.*) Excuse me, is anybody sitting here? (*speaking to Minister*) Oh, hi Pastor. Sorry I'm late.

Minister: That's okay. Make yourself at home. After all, in God's house, it is better to be late than to never arrive at all.

Mike: (*raises hand enthusiastically*) Amen.

Minister: Amen. Let us prepare our hearts for worship as we begin today's service with some special music from our choir . . .

Mike: (*interrupting*) Excuse me!

Minister: Yes, can I help you?

Mike: Can I come up and help with the special music?

Minister: Well, our choir has already prepared something.

Mike: I've heard them practice. They could use another week.

Minister: Well, it does seem that you're being led by the Holy Spirit. Why don't you come up and share with us.

Mike: (*comes up to the stage*) Do you have a guitar?

Minister: (*pointing to a guitar on the stage*) There's one over there nobody ever uses.

Mike: Perfect.

Minister: So, what are you going to share with us today?

Mike: It's an old time favorite. I have really been working hard to get it just right. But I only know one chord.

Minister: One chord?

Mike: Yeah, this one (*plays a very bad chord*)

(*Mike sings the first verse of Amazing Grace off key while strumming the guitar*)

Amazing grace, How sweet the sound,

That saved a wretch like me;

I once was lost, but now am found,

Was blind, but now I see.

Minister: Thank you for that lovely version of Amazing Grace.

Mike: Wait. I can do it another way.

Minister: Another way?

Mike: Yeah. I got this from watching late night TV. This is for people who lived in the 70's.

Minister: People in their 70's?

Mike: (*frustrated*) Not people *in* their 70's. People who *lived* in the 70's.

Minister: Now, didn't people in their 70's live in the 70's?

Mike: (*puzzled look*) Yeah, I guess you're right.

(*sings first verse of Amazing Grace to the tune of The Gilligan's Island Theme*)

Amazing grace, How sweet the sound,

That saved a wretch like me;

I once was lost, but now am found,

Was blind, but now I see.

Minister: Thank you, Gilligan.

Mike: No problem, but I have another way.

Minister: I'm afraid to ask.

Mike: This is for the young people in the audience.

Minister: We do have some of them.

Mike: But I need you to get them clapping.

Minister: You mean, like applause? (*starts applauding*)

Mike: No, you need to get a beat going.

(*Both the Minister and Mike begin clapping to a beat. Mike turns his back to the audience and puts on sunglasses and backward ball cap. He proceeds to sing the first and last verses of Amazing Grace to a rap beat. When completed, he removes his cap and sunglasses and returns to his seat*)

Amazing grace, How sweet the sound,

That saved a wretch like me;

I once was lost, but now am found,

Was blind, but now I see.

Praise God, Praise God, Praise God, Praise God,

Praise God, Praise God, Praise God,

Praise God, Praise God, Praise God, Praise God,

Praise God, Praise God. . . . Praise God.

Minister: Thank you for that inspiring version of Amazing Grace. While we've all been inspired by the music this morning, we're going to move forward with the service, as we don't want to miss out on the beautiful day outside.

Mike: Hey, could you pick up the pace a little bit, Pastor? I have a 1:00 tee time.

Minister: While it's important to sing our praises, it's also important to share our monetary gifts. If I could ask the ushers to come forward at this point . . .

Mike: Excuse me!

Minister: Yes, sir?

Mike: Can I come up and usher?

Minister: Sure, why not. Please, come forward.

(*Mike comes forward*)

Mike: Do you have a collection plate?

Minister: Yes, I've got one right here. (*Minister gets a paper plate from behind lectern and hands it to Mike.*)

Mike: How much do you want?

Minister: I'm sorry, how much do I want?

Mike: Yeah, how much do you want?

Minister: As much as the congregation is led to give.

(*Mike goes through the first few rows of the audience, half-heartedly trying to collect money. After a minute or so of having no luck, he returns the plate to the Minister.*)

Mike: Sorry, Pastor. I didn't have much luck. Looks like you're working for free this week. (*Mike returns to his seat*)

Minister: That's quite alright. It's the thought that counts. (*to the congregation*) At this time, if you would refer to your bulletins, we have a few announcements we'd like to highlight.

Mike: Excuse me!

Minister: (*starting to get a little irritated*) Yes, can I help you?

Mike: Can I come up and read the announcements?

Minister: I don't know, can you read?

Mike: Hey, that wasn't very nice for a pastor.

Minister: You're right. I apologize. Please come forward to read the announcements. But you have to promise to read them just as they're written in the bulletin.

Mike: (*approaches the stage and steps up to the lectern*) I promise to read them just as they're written. Boy, I like helping in church.

Minister: And we appreciate the spirit of helping out. (*hands the bulletin to Mike*)

Mike: (*blows into the microphone*) These are the Sunday announcements! Weight Watchers will be meeting this

Tuesday night at 7:00. Please use the large double doors on the side of the building.

Minister: Um . . .

Mike: You said to read it exactly how it's written.

Minister: I guess I'll have to talk to the secretary about that.

Mike: You do that. Next Saturday, Pastor here will be doing a special sermon titled "What is Hell?" Come early and listen to the choir practice.

Minister: That's supposed to be two separate announcements.

Mike: You better talk to your secretary.

Minister: Would you please continue.

Mike: In two weeks, we will be having our annual rummage sale. Ladies, this is a good chance for you to get rid of all those things you no longer want around the house. Bring your husbands. And these have been our Sunday announcements.

(*Mike returns to his seat.*)

Minister: Thank you. I promise we'll get through this one way or another. (*gets the Bible from the lectern*) Our Scripture reading today is out of the Old Testament. If you would open your Bibles to 2 Kings, Chapter 24, verses 10–12 . . .

Mike: Excuse me!

Minister: (*getting more irritated*) Yes!

Mike: Can I come up and read the Scripture?

Minister: Do you promise to do better than you did with the announcements?

Mike: Well, it is the Word of God.

Minister: You have a good point. I may regret this, but go ahead and come forward.

(*Mike approaches the stage and goes to the lectern. Minister hands him the Bible.*)

Mike: (*speaking into microphone*) Today's Scripture is Two Kings twenty-four, colon, ten dash twelve . . .

Minister: (*interrupting*) You don't need to read the punctuation.

Mike: Okay, thanks.

Minister: Any time.

Mike: At that time the officers of Ne-butch-ad-neez-arrr . . .

Minister: That's Nebuchadnezzar.

Mike: (*softly, as he covers the mic with his hand*) No offense, but how do you get Nebuchadnezzar out of that?

Minister: You're going to have to trust me on this one.

Mike: King of Baby-lawn . . .

Minister: Babylon.

Mike: Advanced on Jerusalem and laid sigh-dge to it.

Minister: Siege! They laid siege to it!

Mike: You say to-may-to, I say to-mah-to.

Minister: Please continue.

Mike: And Ne-butch-ad-neez-arrr himself came up to the city while his officers were be-sigh-dging it . . .

Minister: Besiege. The officers were besieging it!

Mike: Je-ho-ee-atch-en, king of Juh-da . . .

Minister: Judah.

Mike: His mother . . .

Minister: Mother.

Mike: I said mother. I actually got that one right. His atten-dance . . .

Minister: Attendants.

Mike: His nah-bulls . . .

Minister: Nobles.

Mike: And his officials all surrendered to him. Amen. (*Mike returns to seat*)

Minister: (*heavy sigh*) Amen. Moving on to the New Testament

Mike: (*to the person sitting next to him*) Shhh! You're not supposed to laugh at church . . . (*looks up*) Oh, sorry Pastor. Go ahead.

Minister: Our message today comes from the New Testament. We're reading from Romans twelve, colon, six dash— (*gesturing toward Mike in the audience*) Now look, you have me doing it!

Mike: Hey Pastor!

Minister: What!

Mike: Can I help with the message?

Minister: No! This is my message! How are you going to help with my message?

Mike: I can help with the hearing impaired.

Minister: Finally, a noble gift, sign language. Please, come forward and share your gift.

(*Mike comes forward and begins doing hand-stretching exercises*)

Minister: We're reading from Romans 12:6–8. (to Mike) What are you doing?

Mike: I'm warming up.

Minister: Well, I guess that's important, seeing as I don't know anything about sign language. Just let me know when you're ready.

Mike: Okay, I'm ready.

Minister: We all have different gifts . . .

Mike: (*yelling*) We all have different gifts!

Minister: What are you doing?

Mike: (*yelling*) I'm helping the hearing impaired!

Minister: You're going to *make* them hearing impaired.

Mike: (*yelling*) Just continue!

Minister: According to the grace given us.

Mike: (*yelling*) According to the grace given us!

Minister: If a man's gift is prophesying . . .

Mike: (*yelling*) If a man's gift is prophesying!

Minister: Let him do it in proportion to his faith.

Mike: (*yelling*) Let him do it!

Minister: If it is serving . . .

Mike: (*yelling*) If it is serving!

Minister: Let him serve.

Mike: (*yelling*) We already tried that!

Minister: If it is teaching . . .

Mike: (*yelling*) If it is teaching!

Minister: Let him teach.

Mike: (*yelling*) Let him teach!

Minister: If it is encouraging . . .

Mike: (*walks over to the Minister and slaps him on the shoulder, still yelling*) You're doing a heck of a job, Pastor! Two thumbs up! Keep up the good work!

Minister: If it is contributing to the needs of others . . .

Mike: (*pulls out his empty front pants pockets*) Pass.

Minister: If it is leadership . . .

Mike: (*yelling*) If it is leadership!

Minister: Let him govern diligently.

Mike: (*yelling*) Let him govern diligently! (*Pounds fist into his hand*) Owww!

Minister: If it is showing mercy . . .

Mike: (*more softly*) If it is showing mercy!

Minister: Let him do it cheerfully.

Mike: (*smiling and bouncing his head up and down*) Let him do it cheerfully!

Minister: (*walks down to Mike, places the Bible in his hands*) I'll tell you what, son, you seem to have a pretty good handle on this, so I'm going to let you finish today's service.

Mike: You mean . . . you're leaving?

Minister: That's right. The service is all yours. I'm going to take that 1:00 tee time.

(*Minister walks off the stage*)

Mike: Wait a minute. Where are you going? What do I do now? Umm—class dismissed! (*follows the Minister out*)

BIO SKETCH

Mike Webb

Mike had a vision in 1997 to convey the scriptures to people in a light-hearted manner and to show people that Christians can be fun and have joy in their lives. He used his past stand-up comic and theatrical experience to fulfill his mission in life, which is to put a smile on anyone's face by sharing the Word of God to them through humor. Mike handles most of the staging and the business details for the group. When not performing, Mike works in the insurance/accounting field.

Mike and his wife Beth both have degrees in ministry and love serving the Lord through mission work, both local and international, as well as working with youth. Mike and Beth have been married for 17 years and have two children, Josh and Jordan. Mike and his family live in Canal Winchester, Ohio, and attend the Brice United Methodist Church in Columbus, Ohio.

Rick Eichorn

Rick has been a regular member of the Caravan since its inception. He has used his background as a graphic artist to handle the group's promotional and public relations duties. Rick has also taken many of the duo's ideas and put them into a skit format. He does this by taking a humorous look at our daily lives and experiences and applying a message supported by Scripture. His biggest blessing is watching others come to Christ through laughter. Rick works as a customer service supervisor for the City of Columbus.

Rick has been married to his wife Julie for 20 years, and they have three children—Matt, Brittany, and Sarah. Rick and his family live in Pataskala, Ohio, and attend the Community of Faith United Methodist Church in Columbus, Ohio.

For more information regarding The Christian Comedy Caravan's products, merchandise, or to book a ministry performance, please contact us at:

The Christian Comedy Caravan

Email: christiancomedy@insight.rr.com

Or call us at:

614–833–6377 or 740–964–3204

Or visit our website at:

christiancomedycaravan.com